JOHN BROOKES
GARDEN
DESIGN
WORKBOOK

DORLING KINDERSLEY
LONDON · NEW YORK · STUTTGART

A DORLING KINDERSLEY BOOK

First published in Great Britain in 1994
by Dorling Kindersley Limited,
9 Henrietta Street, London WC2E 8PS

A CIP catalogue record for this book is
available from the British Library

ISBN 0 7513 0092 6

Reproduced in Italy by Typongraph
Printed and bound in Italy by Graphicom

CONTENTS

INTRODUCTION

To many people, the very idea of a designed garden is alien. It is perceived as an unnecessary exercise, appropriate only to the gardens of stately homes. The reality is quite different – in fact, the smaller the area, the more it needs a layout to maximize its potential. Plants are seen too often as the *raison d'être* of a garden, and of course they are

Organic shapes
The shapes of plant masses are critical in expressing the harmony and proportion of a garden design.

Design and planting
The combination of design forms in a garden and the textural overlay created by plant material never ceases to intrigue me.

an essential part of it, filling in the pattern, but a designed layout takes into account the function of the space: its paths, changes of level, places to sit, access points, and storage facilities. A garden designer must assess these functions in relation to the house to create a unified garden layout.

It is an odd fact (and any designer will substantiate this) that to design for oneself is far more difficult than to design for someone else; often there are many personal associations with the existing garden to be overcome. The newcomer to garden design may well be doubly confounded – he or she may have all the inhibiting associations, but none of the practical techniques needed to overcome them.

Design details
A good garden design will show sympathetic patterning even down to the details of paving.

The object of my *Garden Design Workbook* is to explain the design process to everyone interested in evolving a garden plan. I will lead you through the design maze step by step, explaining the process as I use it in my own garden design practice and as I teach it at my school.

Before getting to the specifics of garden design, however, and before your eye is trained to discern what is right and what is wrong in terms of shapes, you need to

Natural impact
Bold plants impose their own pattern on a design.

be able to look, see, and enjoy the shapes that are all around us in our daily lives. The practical information in the *Garden Design Workbook* will help you to do this, but you will also have to help yourself by learning to express yourself on paper. Take your pens and paper, abandon inhibitions and prepare to experiment. Do not be afraid to try out fresh ideas: draw graphic shapes, make bold patterns and use colour freely.

Geometric shapes
Experiments with bold, abstract shapes can lead to strong patterns for a garden design.

Bold, linear shapes are only one source of pattern. Naturally occurring patterns are all around us in the veins of leaves, in bark, in landscapes of hills and fields. Learn to see patterns in everything around you, from paving stones to fabrics. Once you get your eye accustomed to recognizing pattern, you will realize that little is random or haphazard. Pattern may be determined by weather, the forces of nature, by man in farming, by machines, and so on. The seemingly random undulation of a landscape seldom occurs without reason, and so kicking a length of hose about in the hope of

Textile patterns
Pattern is everywhere. You can draw inspiration from the graphic patterns of textiles.

The patterns of landscape
Geology, topsoil, flora and climate create natural patterning, modified by the ways we use the land.

The patterns of detail
Close inspection of detail can be inspirational – for example, in drystone walls or cracked earth.

getting inspiration for a "naturalistic" garden pattern will not necessarily be successful. Pattern, and hence design, has a strength and a logic which, I suspect, is why the strong geometry of a formal garden is so attractive to many people.

Geometry, balance and symmetry are qualities we associate with classical orders in architecture and that are to be found in great Renaissance gardens. But from the beginning of the twentieth century we have had another option – that of asymmetry – which can be just as ordered. Abstract, asymmetrical patterns fit far better into the proportions of the average contemporary garden, and give the designer greater flexibility to fulfil the demands of a brief, than rigid classical, formal patterns. Of course, there are, and will always be, situations for which the formal approach remains eminently suitable, and individual elements of classical design can always be used in your garden layout; experiment with moving them about, possibly overlapping them, to create an abstract composition.

Once you have learned to be confident with your pens, pencils, tracing paper overlays and cutouts, you can experiment with design options, entirely in the abstract at first. When you have mastered these skills, I will show you how to relate shapes to the proportions of a house using a basic module or grid.

You then need to relate your pattern to the requirements of a real site. Begin to decide what should go where and why – terracing in sun or shade, a path to the store or garage, places for herbs, to store logs, to hide the compost.

Once you have come to terms with two-dimensional pattern, I will teach you to start thinking in terms of three-dimensional blocks. These blocks will represent different levels of the garden, where appropriate, or different heights of plant material. At this stage, you are still not quite thinking about actual planting; rather you are considering balance and proportion. For ultimately, a garden should be a pleasant place to be in, sheltered from the world between the masses of planting, or looking out on to a fine open view.

A garden design is a three-dimensional project (four-dimensional if you add time and therefore plant growth). I will show you how to move from the two-dimensional plan to the three-dimensional projection. The design concepts of symmetry, asymmetry, abstraction, proportion, dimension and scale may be confusing at first, but in

Symmetry

Asymmetry

Counterpoise

The designer's choices
Just as objects can be arranged to make a pleasing composition on a mantlepiece, so the elements of a garden can be moved around to create a successful design.

Two dimensions
A garden pattern is a collage of shapes – areas of grass, water, paving and planting – that should combine to be visually exciting while functioning on a practical level.

Three dimensions
When heights of structures and plants are added, a two-dimensional scheme takes on three-dimensional reality.

a real design these concepts come to life. Think of the garden designer as a painter putting oil on canvas to represent a scene or a person, or simply to delight the eye by use of colour and texture. Visit an art gallery and examine twentieth-century abstract paintings as well as studying the old masters. The art world is endless in its variety, but you will see how every painter has sought new ways to present us with a very rich library of visual experience – upon which the designer can call. Sculptors too may inspire your garden designs and because they work three-dimensionally, you might feel that their work has even more relevance to the activity of the garden designer, who is also working in these three dimensions.

Learning from artists
Ben Nicolson (1894-1982)
used collage to contrive
extraordinarily
stimulating shapes that
repay close study by
garden designers.

Garden design should not be confused with the craft of gardening. Gardening involves realizing your plan for the site through planting and construction. By thinking too soon about installation and the practical realities of soil and plant material, you will kill the spontaneity of the design process (though eventually, of course, it has to be tempered by all sorts of factors, including financial considerations). But the first stage of garden design, which I wish to share with you in my *Garden Design Workbook*, should be free of all these inhibitions, enabling you to be liberal and ambitious with your ideas.

It is a daunting thought that there are no two identical gardens in the world, for there are no two identical sites. Moreover, because your design vision is exclusive to yourself, your garden design will be a unique creation.

The power of pattern
Asymmetry and geometry
are combined within a
formal framework in this
Bauhaus poster of 1923.

PROPORTION

PROPORTION IN DESIGN means visual balance. In garden design terms it is the art of making a garden sit well within its site, and then of making plant masses, water features, lawns and terraces cohere in a balanced (or proportioned) relationship. A garden looks right only when all its elements are in proportion to each other.

THE IMPORTANCE OF PROPORTION

Well-balanced elements   **Disproportionate** shapes

These illustrations show how shapes in proportion (far left) make a more pleasing design than an unbalanced selection of shapes (left).

USING PROPORTIONAL SHAPES

Correct proportioning is as vital in designing the ground plan as it is in planning heights.

THE GARDEN SPACE
A standard rectangular garden, with fencing and two trees to consider.

GROUND PATTERN SHAPES
The shapes of the ground pattern relate to the scale of the site.

Plant masses

THREE-DIMENSIONAL SHAPES
The plant masses work because they are in proportion to the ground pattern.

THE POWER OF PROPORTION
Simple geometric shapes combine in this garden to create a well-proportioned design.

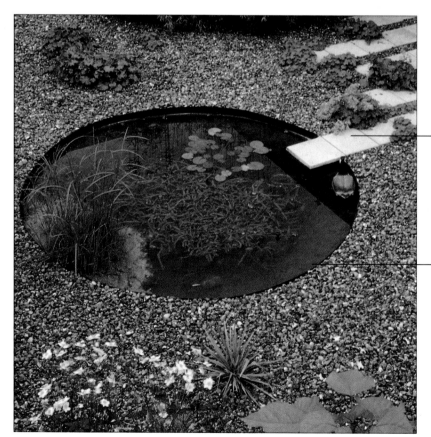

Angled paving slabs juxtapose effectively with the pool

The bold circular pool works successfully in this site because it is balanced in scale by the gravelled area surrounding it

These shapes are bold enough to work visually with the scale of the house and drive

The large shapes of the lawn, paving and drive don't allow the tree to swamp the site

Vertical jet of water contrasts with the horizontals of grass, gravel and planting

The sides of the pool echo the lines of the roof

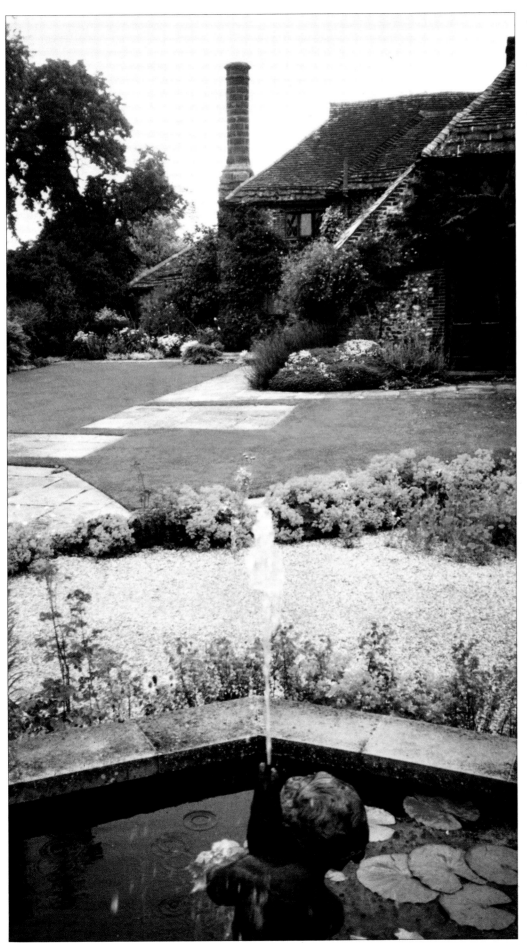

A BALANCED DESIGN
The simplicity of this modern garden design welds the proportion of an older house and surrounding planting both to the entrance drive in the foreground and a neighbouring tree beyond.

PATTERN

ALL GARDEN DESIGNS begin with pattern. In theory, these patterns can take any form you like. In practice, they have to take into account limitations such as awkward corners that are difficult to construct or plants that need a certain width of bed. There will also be aesthetic constraints. To work well, a pattern must be in proportion to the house, the site and its boundaries (see pages 8 and 16). Some believe symmetry to be the essence of a successful pattern, but asymmetry can be just as classic and is less of a straightjacket.

ESTABLISHING A PATTERN

Whether a pattern is symmetrical or not, the shapes within it should always be in proportion.

Guiding grid
(see pp.16-17)

FORMAL PATTERN
This overcomes the site's disproportion.

SYMMETRICAL
Strength derives from balance.

ASYMMETRICAL
This pattern begins to add interest.

ABSTRACT
Moved, the shapes look more subtle.

PRACTICAL
Adding shapes creates a basic plan.

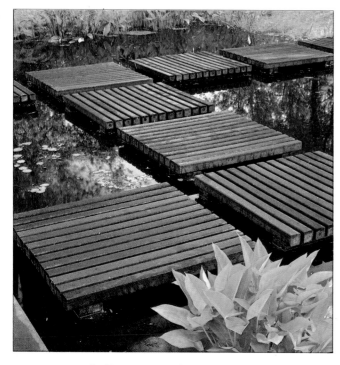

A GEOMETRIC SOLUTION
The simple abstract geometry of timber pads through water leads the eye onward.

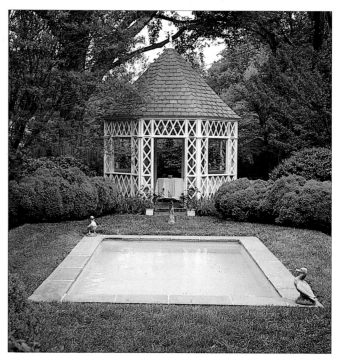

THE CLASSICAL APPROACH
Classic simplicity provides the design answer in one view, although it lacks subtlety.

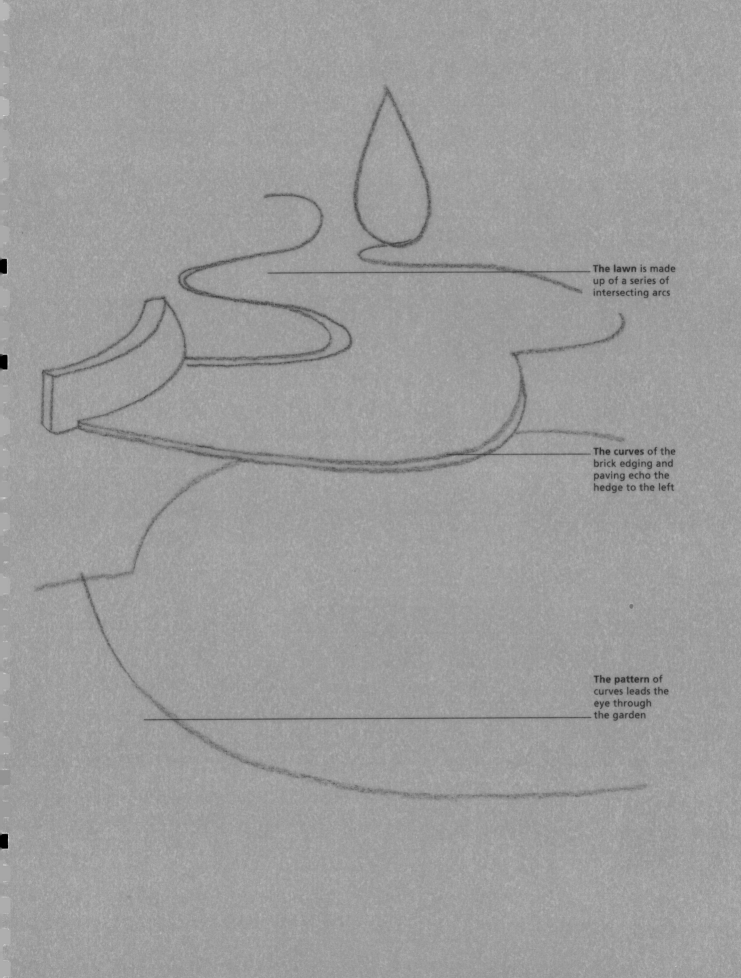

The lawn is made up of a series of intersecting arcs

The curves of the brick edging and paving echo the hedge to the left

The pattern of curves leads the eye through the garden

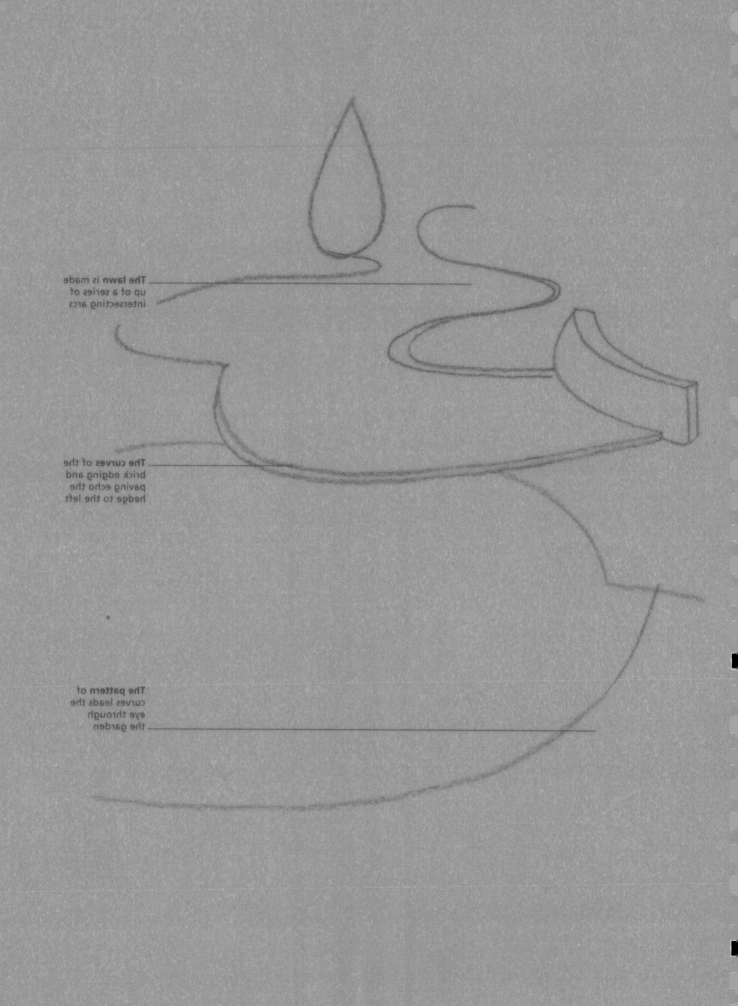

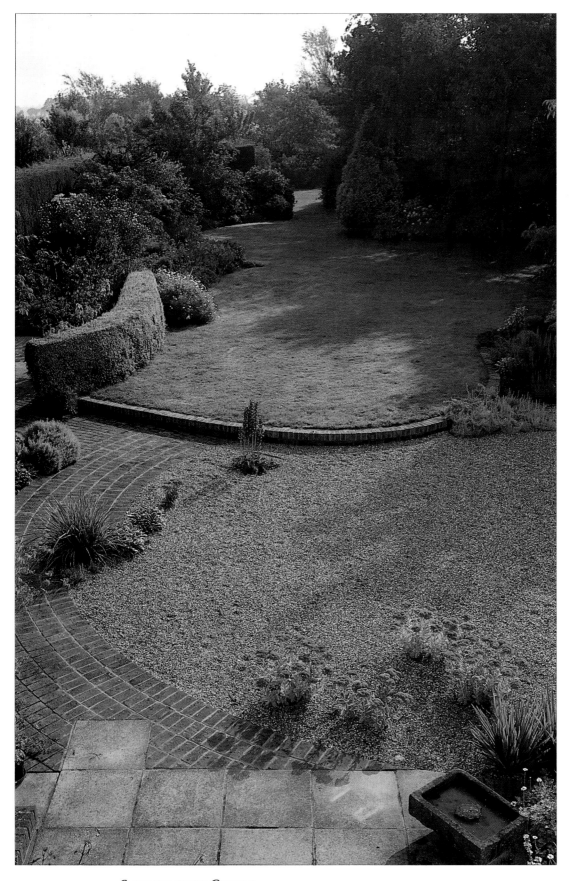

STYLING WITH CURVES

Strong patterns do not have to be angular. Geometric curves
derived from circles and arcs read more strongly within the
shape of a rectangular garden than free-flowing shapes.

MASSES & VOIDS

A WELL-DESIGNED GARDEN is a balance of masses (plants and structures) and voids (the open areas between them). To create harmony between them, you need first to evolve a pattern that is pleasing in itself, then to see if it works in terms of masses and voids.

SIMPLE RELATIONSHIPS

This is a starter exercise to teach you to see patterns as masses and voids.

MAKING THE BASIC SHAPES

Cut out a piece of paper to represent the shape of your garden. Its proportions should be broadly correct, but it does not need to be drawn to scale at this stage.
Then cut out a variety of paper shapes and experiment with them on the paper. The paper shapes you use will be dictated by your sense of style; the way you arrange them will derive from what feels right to you. Remember: you are making patterns and thinking about shapes, not planning your own garden yet.

Garden shape

Paper shapes

DESIGN TIPS

◆ Put aside the drawbacks of your own garden for a moment. Think of it as just an empty space that you can fill with any shapes you choose.

◆ The first stage of design has nothing to do with horticulture and everything to do with making space work in a visually satisfying way.

GOOD PATTERN, POOR DESIGN

This pattern is harmonious, but does not work as masses and voids – there is no space (void) adjacent to the house.

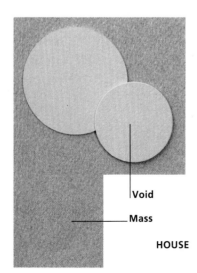

Void

Mass

HOUSE

A BETTER USE OF SPACE

A bolder approach, this pattern uses more of the plot's area, but creates some uncomfortable angles.

Awkward gaps need to be resolved

HOUSE

A POWERFUL SOLUTION

A strong design: the overlap between the octagon shapes makes a focal point to be developed.

Focal point

Octagons overlying rectangles

HOUSE

TRANSLATING PATTERNS INTO MASSES AND VOIDS

The simplest patterns, translated into masses and voids, can yield graphic results.

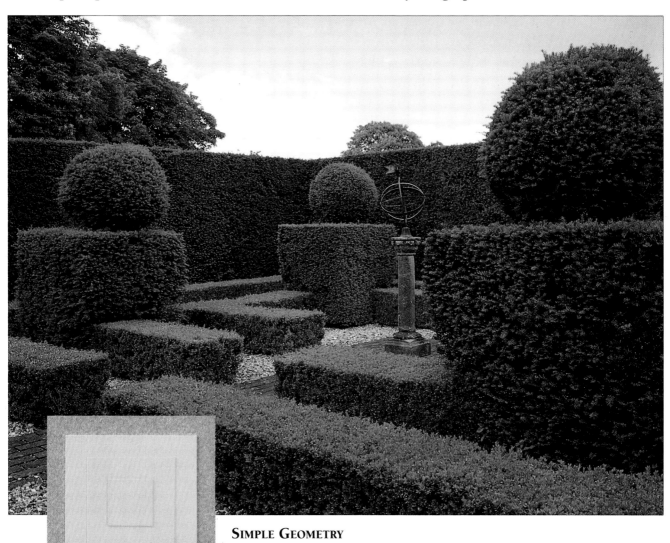

SIMPLE GEOMETRY
The initial plan for this splendidly formal garden is no more than three concentric squares.

AN EXPERIMENT WITH CIRCLES
Three circles are all that comprise this pattern (right), in which the two large circles provide balance and the smaller one movement. The challenge is to make them work as masses and voids.

When it is projected (far right), the two circles are linked to make one space. The design emerges as a fluent sequence of curves, making excellent use of the available space.

Plan

Projection

Void

Void

Mass

Mass

13

WHY USE A GRID?

THE FACADES OF MOST HOUSES are designed with proportion in mind. The architect plans the structure on units or modules of space which may reflect the scale of the rooms. If the garden designer can plan the garden using the same module as the architect – or a proportion of it, perhaps half or double – the house and garden will fit well together visually.

PRACTICAL TIPS

- Look for the strongest feature on the house, such as a bay, then see how its proportions relate to the rest of the façade.
- If there is no dominant feature, look for the rhythm of doors and windows.

FINDING A RHYTHM

Even the flat façade of a house will have a rhythm of windows and doors that you can analyse.

Sliding window

Divisions do not have to align exactly with the house

SIMPLE DIVISIONS

The large sliding window on the left is the dominant feature of this façade. See how the rest of the house can be divided using the same module.

A STRICT PATTERN

This asymmetrical house is designed to a strict proportion based on the width of the bay. Halving this module gives a workable grid for the garden.

Bay

A HIDDEN MODULE

The bay dominates the façade of this house, but its width is not repeated as a whole unit. Halve the bay's width, however, and you discover the rhythm of the construction on which to base a grid.

TURNING THE GRID

This elegant façade could have a module of four or five squares. By turning the resulting grid at 45°, the attached building is tied into the overall plan and the proportion is retained.

Grid turned at 45°

The shapes of planting, lawn and paving are all planned using the grid as a guide

Grid square based on the structure of the house

The shapes of planting, lawn and paving are all planned using the grid as a guide

Grid square based on the structure of the house

ENLARGING THE GRID

Increasing the size of the grid square – doubling or quadrupling it as you approach the far boundaries of the garden – ensures that the ensuing pattern will relate to larger elements outside the site.

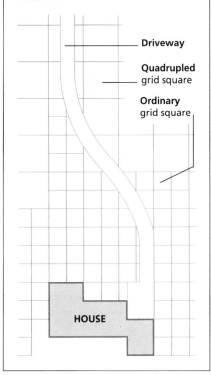

Driveway

Quadrupled grid square

Ordinary grid square

HOUSE

THE GRID IN ACTION

In this "live" example, the lines on the tracing paper overlay demonstrate how the basic grid square has been based on the rhythm of windows and door on the house. The same grid is then extended over the garden.

FROM GRID TO GARDEN

THE OWNERS OF THE STYLISH PERIOD HOUSE shown on page 15 wanted their garden to be divided into three units: a hard-surfaced, contained area near the house where the dog could be left safely outside when the owners were out, a middle "garden" area, and a paved terrace at the end, overlooking the river. The garden is long and narrow, and already has a built-up terrace at the river end. The rhythm of the house is easy to establish: there are three units, expressed as door, window, window on the ground floor, and as three windows on the floor above. This gives a grid module which is one-third of the width of the house.

Retaining wall to end terrace

Six grid squares

The central shapes are adjusted to accommodate existing planting

Overlapping blocks create a harmonious effect

Sculpture or statue to punctuate length of garden

This shape echoes the block at the end of the site

Six grid squares

River terrace

Terrace for dog near the house

Steps

Basement area

Basement area

HOUSE

SETTING UP
The plan is turned so that the designer can work as if looking into the site from the house. Then the grid is drawn ready for use. The horizontal lines of the grid are drawn starting from the basement.

MAKING BLOCKS
Multiples of the grid squares can be experimented with. These are the building blocks and can be used to make patterns. The grid itself can now be abandoned: the blocks contain the correct proportions.

THE DESIGN
The rigid geometry of the building blocks has been modified to accommodate existing planting, but the design remains essentially true to the proportions of the blocks, and so to the proportions of the house.

The areas near the house remain uncluttered by planting, balancing the bold masses of plants in the area beyond

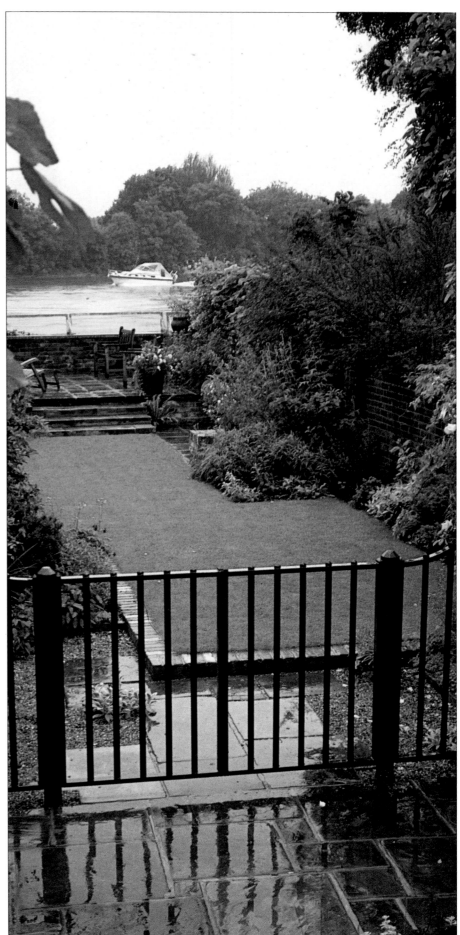

THE GRID AND THE GARDEN

The grid has been laid over the garden and it is now possible to see how the ground pattern was arrived at. The structural essentials, including the steps, back wall and raised terrace, have been drawn in so that their relationship to the grid can also be seen.

THE THIRD DIMENSION

The scale and shape of plant masses give the central part of the site unity, yet link visually with the terraces. The shapes of the plant masses, as conceived in bold blocks, are shown on the tracing paper overlay.

EQUIPMENT & DRAFTING SKILLS

GARDEN DESIGN IDEAS will only be accurate on site if they are planned with precision and are in proportion from the outset. With practice, patience and care, anyone can produce competent working garden drawings, but some simple equipment is needed.

ESSENTIAL EQUIPMENT

The equipment you need to draw garden plans is all standard and readily available from art shops.

THE DRAWING BOARD

Drawing boards should be at least 1m (3ft) wide and the angle should be adjustable. Some models have useful "parallel motion" rulers attached.

Pencils
Use HB grade for drafting, 2B (softer) for sketching, and 2H (medium hard) for precise scale drawing

Pencil sharpener   **Eraser**

HB pencil

2B pencil

2H pencil

Fine point
fibre-tipped pen for finishing drawings

Marker pens in light landscape colours for colouring in masses

A scale rule is indispensable. The units of measurement on the rule make it easy to transpose the measurements of your site on to your scale drawing.

45° triangle

60° triangle

Compasses

90°

90°   60°

45°

Masking tape
to hold drawings securely on the board

Craft knife for scratching out inked lines

Circle templates
are quicker to use than setting compasses, but may not include the precise radius you need

BASIC DRAFTING SKILLS

Accurate drawing abilities and a sharp pencil are the prerequisites for drafting working plans.

THE CENTRE OF A SQUARE
Draw a horizontal line and measure it. With a 45° triangle draw vertical lines of the same length from either end. Join them. Draw two diagonals with the triangle to link the opposite corners. Where they cross is the centre.

DRAWING CIRCLES IN SQUARES
Draw a square as shown, left, and where the diagonal lines cross is its centre. Put the compass point on the intersection, spread the compasses to reach the nearest part of the square and draw a circle.

SUBDIVIDING SQUARES
Draw a square and its diagonals, then make a vertical line and a horizontal line through the centre. Draw diagonal lines in the four smaller squares you have made to find their centres and draw a circle in each.

TYPES OF PAPER

Through all the stages of a developing garden plan use tracing paper – it allows you to make overlays and see through the different layers. If your drawing board is other than white, put white card behind the paper. Use the lightest weight tracing paper for your early workings and a heavier weight, preferably 90 gsm, for the final drawing.

DESIGNING WITH SHAPES
When you can draw the basic shapes described above, use them as units to compile complex forms. Experiment by turning your tracings and setting them at various angles. Create further possibilities by overlaying more tracings in different colours.

HOW TO MEASURE

ACCURATE MEASUREMENT of the site is the essential first stage in designing a new garden. It is not difficult, though it does require care. Draw the outline of your garden freehand on a clipboard pad, then record all the measurements you make of the site on this rough plan, following the advice given here. You will then be ready to make a scaled drawing that will be the starting point for any subsequent design.

HB pencil and sharpener

Fabric tape measure 30m (100ft) or longer

Clipboard and paper

Pegs to hold tape and mark offsets

THE EQUIPMENT
Fabric tape measures are preferable to metal ones, which have sharp edges and can rust. Meat skewers make a good alternative to wooden pegs.

THE FIRST STAGES

First measure the house, noting the positions of doors and windows.

Tree

Paved area

Lawn

The house and garden

Flower bed

ROUGH PLAN OF THE SITE
To make a rough plan, go into the garden with the equipment shown above. You will need to measure all boundaries, the house (including doors and windows), flower beds and so on. Use a peg to hold one end of the tape. To position fixed features such as trees and manhole covers, you need to take offsets (see facing page). Record your detailed measurements as on the plan shown.

Window

HOUSE

Window

Tree

Running measurements aligning with house features

Door

Lawn

Paved area

Flower bed

Manhole cover

MAKING A WORKING SKETCH

As you take each measurement, record it on the rough plan on your clipboard. Virtually all houses have 90°corners and most boundaries lead away from the house at right angles, but even when things look square, measure to check.

HOUSE

Tree

Offset

Measuring
tape

Peg

Peg

Offset

Manhole cover | Record these lengths

Triangulation lines establish position of tree

HOUSE

Triangulation lines establish corner of garden

RECORDING OFFSETS

To establish positions of features such as trees and manhole covers while measuring, note the exact position of your tape while it is laid across the garden. Place pegs beside the tape opposite features whose positions you wish to determine. Measure from the start of the tape to each peg. Then measure the distances from the pegs to the features. These measurements are known as offsets. Their accuracy can be checked by triangulating (see opposite).

TRIANGULATING

To record the exact position of a fixed object such as a corner of the garden or a tree, measure it from two points on the house.

Tree

HOUSE

Running measurements across width of garden

Offsets | Flower bed

DEFINING CURVES

Take 90° offsets (as above) at regular intervals – say every 1m (3ft) – to record the general shape of curves such as in a flower bed or lawn. Mark each measurement and join the points freehand.

DRAWING TO SCALE

ONCE THE SITE HAS BEEN MEASURED UP and you have entered the dimensions on the rough plan, it is time to make a scale drawing of the plot. Choose a scale that will allow you to get the entire drawing on one piece of tracing paper that will fit on your drawing board. Use a sharp 2H pencil: it is important to be as accurate as possible. You can thicken up certain lines later (see facing page).

CHOOSING A SCALE

- ◆ Use a scale of 1:100 for medium-sized and larger gardens. That means 1cm (or 1 inch) on the rule represents 1m (or 100 inches) on the ground. This scale is also suitable for showing tree planting plans.
- ◆ Use a scale of 1:50 for the plan of a small garden or to make a scale drawing of planting details.
- ◆ A scale of 1:20 is useful for showing details such as a flight of steps.

MAKING THE PLAN

Start by taping a piece of tracing paper on to your drawing board.

The raw material for your scale drawing is your freehand rough plan with all dimensions recorded (see page 20).

1 START WITH THE HOUSE
Rule a horizontal line, then draw to scale the shape of the back/front/sides of the house, as appropriate. Mark positions of windows, doors, bays and recesses.

2 DEVELOP THE OUTLINES
Draw right angles where they occur and establish the outlines of the plot and garden buildings. Measure lines to scale. Join positions to fill in house detail.

3 TRANSFERRING OFFSETS
Mark on the plan where you had placed your tape. Record the peg points, then measure off at 90° to position the features.

4 TRIANGULATED POINTS
Set the compass to the scaled measurement. Work from the point of triangulation and draw arcs. The feature is where they intersect.

EQUIPMENT NEEDED

Drawing board ◆ tape ◆ tracing paper ◆ triangle(s) ◆ scale or ordinary ruler ◆ 2H pencil ◆ sharpener ◆ compass ◆ eraser ◆ pen to finish drawing

SHOWING DETAILS
These are standard ways to illustrate the commonest garden features when adding detail to plans.

Brick

Slab paving

Stone paving

Gravel

Proposed trees

Shrubs

5 FINISHING OFF
To make the plan easy to understand, draw a circle to represent the radius of tree spread, draw slabs in the paved area (see above right), join up offset marks to give the border its shape and locate the manhole.

HOUSE

Existing trees can be represented by an unbroken circle. Proposed trees may be shown with a broken line.

Thicker lines make positions of buildings obvious

Paved area

Mown grass can be represented by a plain green wash. Add dots to show rough grass.

PROFESSIONAL TOUCHES
Inking over the pencil lines and using a thicker pen for house walls gives the plan an immediate lift. Colouring the lawn and paved area adds vitality.

Flower bed

Manhole cover

BRINGING THE PLAN TO LIFE

A WELL-FINISHED SCALE PLAN is essential, but there are times when it does not show clearly all you would like to see. It gives you no idea, for example, of heights of proposed structures or plants and therefore little sense of what the garden will look like to someone in it. There are several kinds of drawing that can be used to develop your scale plan. Sections and elevations establish heights and relationships between them; a projection does a similar job from a different angle; and perspective drawings add a realistic quality.

SCALE PLAN
All the proposed structures and main plantings on the site appear on a finished plan, but this gives you no idea of their heights. To establish these factors you need to draw an elevation (below) or a projection (facing page).

Upper pool

Waterspill

Lower pool

Section line
(see page 27)

Planter

Gravelled area

Seat

Trellis

Elevation line
(see page 26)

Perspective view

Planter

Projection view

An elevation

Neighbouring building, taken into account in the design, will not show on the plan

A section   Upper pool   Lower pool

Planter

Upper pool

Planters   Lower pool

SECTIONS & ELEVATIONS
A section is a slice through a garden and is very useful for planning the details of construction. An elevation helps you to establish the relationships between different elements in the garden. The techniques for drawing both are similar and are shown on pages 26–27.

Upper pool

Lower pool

Seat

DRAWING OVER A PHOTOGRAPH

This is an easy way to try out ideas for new structures and larger plantings. Work on tracing paper taped over a photograph of your garden.

Planter

PROJECTION

This is the view as it would appear from a next door upstairs window. See pages 28–29 for the technique.

The principle ruling perspective drawing is that all lines converge on a notional vanishing point

Loose planting in gravel

Gravelled area

Vanishing point

Picture plane

Eye line

PERSPECTIVE DRAWING

This method of drawing gives a dynamic impression of a design proposal, though it gives you none of the information you need for construction and does require some drawing skill. The alternative, if you are not confident about your drawing, is to draw over a photograph, using the camera's ready-made perspective, as shown above.

ELEVATIONS & SECTIONS

AN ELEVATION GIVES A UNIQUE VIEW of the way plant masses and structures in a plan will interrelate. Planning and plotting the height of each element gives a preview of the finished garden from ground level. A section is a slice through a garden made using similar techniques.

EQUIPMENT NEEDED

Drawing board ◆ scale rule or ordinary ruler ◆ tracing paper ◆ tape ◆ large triangle ◆ pencil ◆ sharpener ◆ eraser ◆ fibre-tipped pen to finish the drawings

MAKING AN ELEVATION

Tape your scale plan on the drawing board and place tracing paper over it. Now decide how much of the garden you wish to show in your elevation.

Line for section

Line for elevation

CHOOSING A LINE
The green line is where the elevation will be taken from. Only features above it will appear in the drawing. The red line will be used to develop a section (see facing page).

1 MAKE THE FIRST LINES
Draw a horizontal line clear of the top of the plan. This is the base line of your elevation. Draw in the heights of any existing walls or structures which may affect your final design. Then, working up from the elevation (green) line, draw vertical lines up through the intersections of the lines on the plan. These vertical lines should extend above the base line: lengthen or shorten them as you decide on the heights of new structures.

Back wall of elevation

Base line for elevation

Wall – scale plan ends here

Vertical lines drawn up from intersections on the plan

Upper pool

Lower pool

Planter

Seat

Vertical lines joined to show height of planter

THE FINISHED ELEVATION

For a really convincing elevation, add freehand features such as the building which, though it does not appear on the plan, will affect the garden's appearance. Draw in major plant masses to add realism.

This building does not show on the plan because it is outside the garden

2 MEASURE HEIGHTS

Working to scale, decide on and measure off the heights of the structures, then join the verticals. For a professional result, copy your elevation on to plain paper, ink over it and add details in pen.

Base line for section drawing

Section line

TAKING A SECTION

Sections (or cross-sections) are slices through a design. Their main use is to clarify details prior to construction.

1 DRAW A SECTION LINE

Select the part of the garden through which you wish to take a cross-section and draw a line across it – in this case, the red line on the plan (see facing page). This is the section line. Draw in a base line above the plan. Draw vertical lines up from the section line just as you would when making an elevation.

Garden wall | Planter wall | Lower pool wall | Garden wall

2 ESTABLISH HEIGHTS

Decide on and mark heights of structures on the verticals. Join these marks with horizontals.

THE FINISHED SECTION

By revealing the proposed heights of structures, a section can serve as a design check before building.

Back wall

Planter   Lower pool

Upper pool

PROJECTING A PLAN

THE VALUE OF DRAWING A PROJECTION is that it enables you to visualize in three dimensions (length, breadth and height) what you have designed on a plan. A projection works only when you have structures – plants are difficult to draw from this aerial angle. What you achieve is the view from next door's upstairs window. Remember to draw heights to the same scale as ground dimensions.

EQUIPMENT NEEDED

Drawing board ◆ large triangle ◆ tracing paper
tape ◆ pencil ◆ sharpener ◆ eraser ◆ sharp blade ◆
pens to finish the drawing

Planters · Pools · Seat · Back wall · Gravel

THE PLAN
This shows a proposal for adding planters, a seat and linked pools to a garden. If you find it hard to visualize the built result, follow steps 1 to 6 to draw a projection.

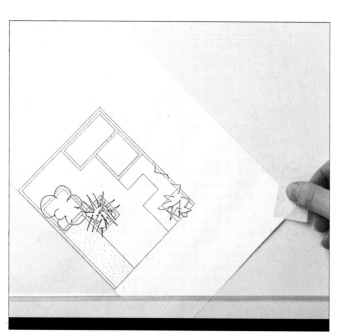

DRAWING A PROJECTION

A projection is like a pop-up plan and will make your garden plan come alive.

1 POSITION THE PLAN
Use a triangle to position the plan at a 45° angle to the parallel motion rule on your board. Tape down.

2 OVERLAY TRACING PAPER
Put your tracing paper at right angles to the rule and tape it down. Using a triangle, trace the outline of your plan in pencil.

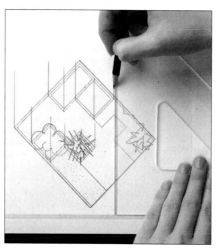

3 DRAW UP VERTICALS
Using a triangle to keep your lines at 90° to the rule, draw vertical lines up from each point of intersection on the plan.

4 MARK OFF HEIGHTS
Measure and mark the different heights, working to the same scale as the plan. Then join up the lines you have projected.

6 CLEAN UP
Erase surplus pencil lines and scrape off unwanted ink lines with a blade – the finished projection should be crisp. If you wish to add detail to produce full renderings like those shown below, make photocopies to work on.

5 INK IN
The design comes alive as you draw over your pencil lines with a pen. Remove the original plan first and substitute a sheet of white paper as background.

PROJECTING A CYLINDRICAL SHAPE
Draw a circle. Mark points on it. Decide on the height of the shape, measure up from each point and make another set of marks. Join these to create an identical circle.

A COLOURED PROJECTION
A projection looks more realistic if details such as plant shapes and paving are inked in and coloured.

Water effects are made by creating a texture on the blue surface colour

Planting is indicated by simple coloured shapes

Dots represent a gravelled area

CASE STUDY: A COUNTRY GARDEN

TWO ADJOINING COTTAGES in a village had been knocked into one house, and the new owners wanted the gardens to be replanned. The rear of the "new" house has a sunny aspect and looks uphill toward an old cherry orchard. From the top of the site there is a wonderful view down over the house. A sunken road runs beside the garden and this will need to be screened.

BEFORE THE SURVEY

I walked around the site to get an idea of its possibilities.

THE BUILDING STYLE
The house (shown right) is built of mellow stone in a traditional cottage style.

THE GARDEN AS I FOUND IT
This is the main part of the garden, with the road running alongside. The house is off to the right.

Neighbouring house

Sunken road

Orchard
House
Lane

THE LOCATION
The village is a farming community with most houses backing on to open country.

QUESTIONNAIRE

Before you begin to plan a garden there are some basic questions you should ask yourself (or the owner). The questions that follow are those I asked the owners of the garden I am about to replan.

Q Are you keen gardeners? Do you have any preferences about features and types of plant?

A *We like to garden, but it is not our only leisure activity and we are not plant specialists. We would, however, like you to plan a pool and a rose bed.*

Q To remake a site this large is a sizeable task. The design must be completed in one go, but would you prefer to implement it in stages?

A *It makes sense to us to reshape the garden in phases, with the court-yard at the rear of the house being remade first.*

Q Do you have any specific requirements that I should bear in mind while designing your garden?

A *No, not particularly. What we would like is a garden that is suitable for most purposes – and especially for outdoor entertaining.*

LOOKING FOR POSSIBILITIES

I established where the best views are and found the most agreeable places to make seating areas.

THE INITIAL SKETCH
My first sketch records the main features of the site that I will not be able to alter.

PRACTICAL TIPS
- On your first rough plan record sunny, shady and windy areas.
- Note neighbouring buildings, trees and features that are seen from the garden.
- Note soil type(s) and local materials.

Strong winds

Steps up from parking

direction of Sun

border

view up to cherry orchard

store

roses

roses

Sunken area

partly shaded

house

juniper

Side lane below wall

border

amazing views

Sunny

Sloping grass

retain view this way

weeping willow (keep)

Phone box

ash

stile

good buildings

fruit tree (keep)

road 2m below garden level

Screen

SITE SURVEY

MAKE A DETAILED SURVEY at the outset. You will need it very soon and there is no better discipline to make you look closely at every aspect of the site. Make enlarged drawings of individual areas if you cannot fit detailed dimensions on your main plan.

FIRST MEASUREMENTS
I plotted the house accurately within the site and measured the boundaries (see pages 20–21).

Outbuildings · **Courtyard** · **HOUSE**

Steps to orchard

16m (52ft) · 24m (79ft) · 8.5m (28ft) · 21m (69ft) · 35m (115ft) · 47m (154ft) · 25m (82ft) · Tree

TAKING OFFSETS
I took offsets (see page 21) to establish the positions of trees that I thought I might keep.

Outbuildings · **Courtyard** · **HOUSE** · **Offsets**

Tree · 14m (46ft) · 19.5m (64ft) · 10m (33ft) · 10m (33ft) · 25m (82ft) · 23m (75ft) · 18m (59ft) · 29m (95ft)

12.5m (41ft) · **Steps** · 13m (43ft) · 7m (23ft) · 5.5m (18ft)

Courtyard

Door · **Window** · **Window** · **Door**

13m (43ft) · 10.5m (35ft) · 7.5m (25ft) · 3m (10ft)

HOUSE

RECORDING DETAILS
Separate, larger-scale drawings are needed to record measurements of complex areas such as this courtyard. It is important to mark the positions of doors, windows, manholes and any other features.

**Quartered
squares** will
allow me to
design this
area in finer
detail but still
using a grid

The main unit
of the grid
based on the
combined
width of a
door and
a bay

Quartered squares will allow me to design this area in finer detail but still using a grid

The main unit of the grid based on the combined width of a door and a bay

CHOOSING THE GRID

The back of the house has a visual rhythm of door–bay–bay–door that divides the façade into four equal elements. I shall use this as the basis of my grid, though I can foresee it will need adapting for the courtyard area (see pages 14–15).

QUARTERING THE SQUARES

The grid squares are unwieldy in relation to the courtyard. To give myself more flexibility I quartered them.

DRAWING GRIDS

To work as I have done here, lay tracing paper over your survey and draw the first lines of the grid, which are those that divide the house. The distance between these lines gives you the size of the grid square so that you can complete the square. Extend the grid until it covers the entire plan.

The scale plan

Outbuildings

Door
Bay

HOUSE

Courtyard

Bay

Door

| 0 | 6 | 12 | 18 | 24 | 30 | ft |
| 0 | 2 | 4 | 6 | 8 | 10 | m |

PLANNING THE COURTYARD

THE COURTYARD IS THE CORE of this garden, and the obvious place to start; the rest of the design will develop from it. I decided to give the courtyard a strong centre. Using quartered grid squares (see page 33) enabled me to experiment with shapes, while bearing in mind the practicalities of access.

The house is at the side on the survey

I turned the plan 90° to design the courtyard

FIRST THOUGHTS
This design allows easy access to the house, the out-buildings, the path round the side of the house and the steps to the garden's upper level. It is practical, but dull.

SECOND THOUGHTS
By cutting up the design further, I was able to create a complex, symmetrical pattern. This was interesting, but altogether too grand for the style of the house.

RETHINKING
I have got rid of the over-formal pattern and made access to the buildings, path and steps easier. An improvement: it is clean and focused, but still unexciting.

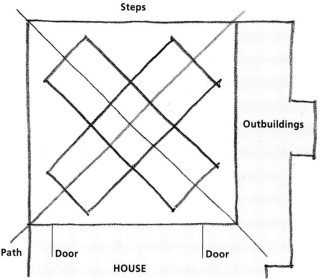

NEAR A SOLUTION
I turned the grid 45°. This results in some odd corners and no circulatory system as yet, but is interesting. I will try joining the outer corners of the cross shape.

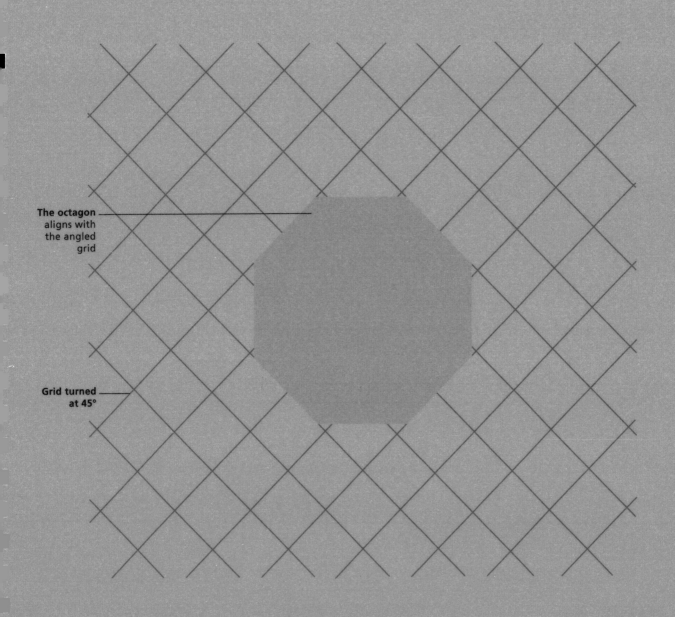

The octagon aligns with the angled grid

Grid turned at 45°

FROM CONCEPT TO COMPLETION

The cross shape is transformed into an octagon which allows a focal point in the centre, easy access all round and planting against the walls.

A PROFESSIONAL TOUCH

To plan a feature such as this octagonal courtyard it is a great help if the grid is angled through 45°. This produces diagonal lines with which to align the edges of the octagon.

0   3   6   9   12   ft
0   1   2   3   4   m

Steps to upper level

Pathway

Planting against outbuilding walls

Outbuildings

Easy access around house doors

Planting against house wall

Path

HOUSE

DETAILING THE DESIGN

Having determined the size of the central octagon, I drew this sketch to show my design for the steps that are needed to compensate for changes in level.

THE FINISHED COURTYARD

With the construction stage completed, I can now confirm that the two pairs of steps work well, changing the gentle slope of the courtyard into clearly defined levels.

DEVELOPING THE DESIGN

NOW THAT I HAVE RESOLVED the pattern of the courtyard, it is time to extend the concept over the rest of the site, experimenting with octagons, diagonals and right angles. The courtyard pattern arose when I turned the grid at 45° to the house, and I will keep the grid at this angle for the rest of the garden.

REMEMBERING THE BRIEF

The garden designer should no longer work in the abstract, but plan specific garden features that will work with the limitations of the site, so I refer back to the site survey and lay the grid over it.

Grid laid over site survey

Outbuildings

Courtyard

HOUSE

Long aspect
to summerhouse

Outbuildings

Long
border

Courtyard

HOUSE

Upper
lawn

Existing tree
in rough grass

Small orchard

Shrub screen

Summerhouse
and pool area

ANGLING THE GRID
I taped down the site survey with the grid laid across it at 45°, as with the courtyard. I reduced the courtyard design to the scale of the plan.

USING THE GRID'S ANGLES
Following the grid lines, I used the combination of diagonals and right angles that make up the courtyard design to define other areas of the garden (see left).

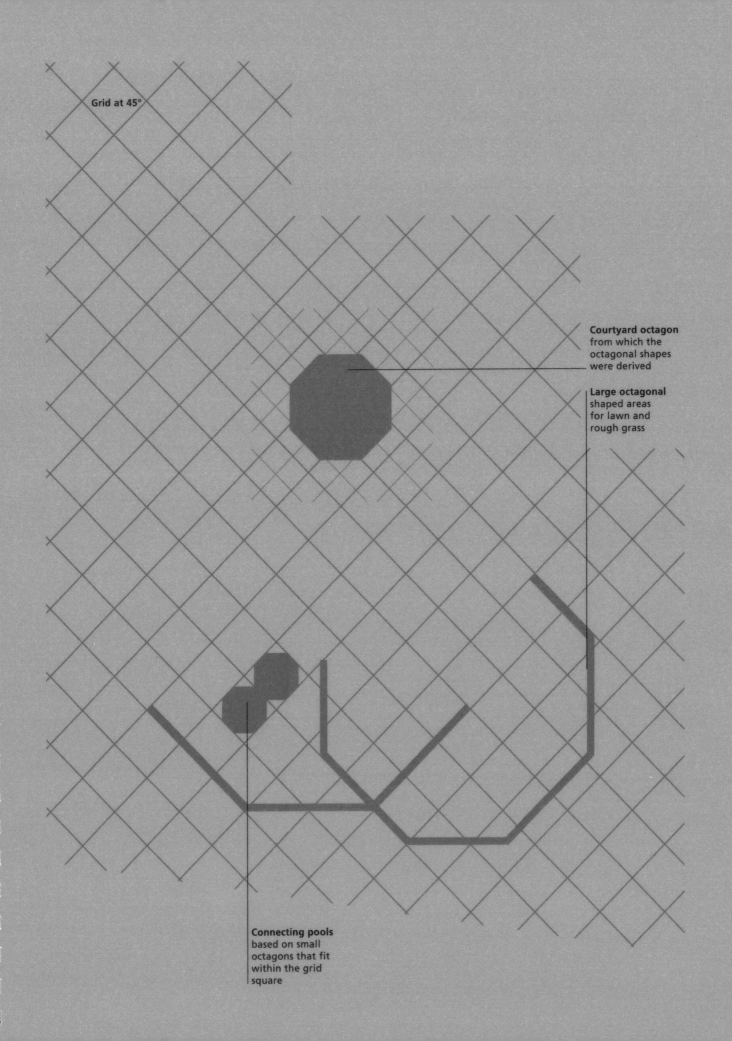

Grid at 45°

Courtyard octagon
from which the
octagonal shapes
were derived

Large octagonal
shaped areas
for lawn and
rough grass

Connecting pools
based on small
octagons that fit
within the grid
square

THE SKELETON DESIGN

I enlarged the octagon shape to supply the general pattern for the garden and reduced it to give shape to the rose garden, summerhouse and connecting pools. The grid used is shown on the tracing paper overlay.

0   6   12   18   24   30   ft

0   2   4   6   8   10   m

Outbuildings

Grassed walk

HOUSE

Long border

Rose garden

Screen planting against road

Lower lawn

Summerhouse

Screen planting

Existing tree

CHOOSING A STYLE

THE SHAPES YOU USE in a design should make the plan work for those who use the garden, but it is the styling of that design that makes the garden fit into its location. Plants are a major factor, but so are the choice of materials for paving and walling, the style of garden buildings and the choice of garden furniture. All these elements should be in harmony with each other, and with the house and its wider location.

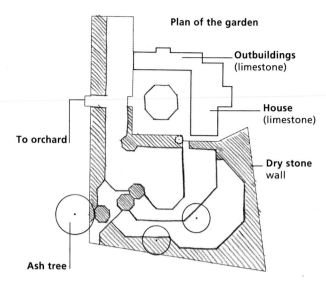

Plan of the garden

Outbuildings (limestone)

House (limestone)

To orchard

Dry stone wall

Ash tree

PAVING AND WALLING

Select building materials that harmonize with the house and local tradition. Look at neighbouring examples to help you decide on details of construction. For this case study garden, dry stone walling was the natural choice to match the limestone of adjacent buildings.

Sawn sandstone

Dressed sandstone

Limestone

Irregular paving

Concrete textures

Artificial stone

STYLES OF FENCING

Fences in town are used to screen out the neighbours and act as a form of security and are therefore likely to be solid. In the country, their purpose is to restrict animals, so open styles are adequate, perhaps modified with chicken wire where necessary.

Picket fencing

Woven fencing

GARDEN STRUCTURES

These should always be built to
suit the house and the local style
as far as possible. In this case
study, the architect based the
shape of the summerhouse (see
page 43) on the form of an
adjacent building and chose
limestone to blend in with
the surrounding structures.

CONTAINERS

Choose containers that have simple
but pleasing outlines and are made in
materials that are sympathetic to the
surroundings. In a cottage garden,
such as this, classical urns
would be incongruous.

Unglazed container

Baskets can be painted
or left plain, but need
to be lined

Studio pots are decorative
in their own right

Terracotta pots
should be frostproof

Wooden half-barrels
must be kept damp

GARDEN FURNITURE

Both appearance and comfort matter
when you choose furniture. Classic,
simple benches and tables look good
anywhere, but beware vibrant
colours. Darker shades of paint and
stain or plain, natural wood are more
appropriate in a country setting.

Elegant seating suits larger gardens

Single chairs are
easier to move
than benches

Folding tables store
away in winter

Simple forms work
best in most gardens

VISUALIZING THE DESIGN

EVEN IF YOU HAVE a firm idea of what you want when designing your own garden, it is a good idea to sketch key areas and features to establish the concepts that guided the plan. Notice that open spaces (in this case lawns) are as important as planted spaces; I aim to create a visual balance between them.

FOCAL POINTS
There are two such features: the sundial in the centre of the sunken courtyard, and the summerhouse.

THE SUMMERHOUSE
This terminates the mixed border and grass walk. It also echoes the roof lines of buildings beyond the site.

THE COURTYARD
This is how the courtyard and house will look seen from the summerhouse across the twin pools.

THE OUTLINE DESIGN
Still an outline, since it lacks planting details and constructional drawings, the plan shows how the different elements such as areas of planting and hard surfacing interrelate at ground level.

0 6 12 18 24 30   ft
0   2   4   6   8   10 m

Brick paving
of the steps in the courtyard

Grass walk

Steps up from parking area

Outbuildings

Courtyard
octagonal lawn

HOUSE

Steps up from court-yard to grass walk

Mixed planting in long border

Steps up to orchard

Sundial

Rose bed

Small trees in rough grass

Shrub planting

Traditional dry stone construction is used for retaining walls

Lawn upper level

Lawn lower level

Hard surfacing

Existing tree

Summerhouse

Stile

Upper pool

Lower pool

Weeping willow retained

Screen planting against road beyond

The twin pools, showing the waterspill, or overflow

PLANNING TO BUILD

I DESIGNED THE LINKED OCTAGONAL POOLS to work with the summerhouse, which is also octagonal, strengthening the visual theme set in the courtyard. The upper pool is raised, whereas the lower pool is just below ground level. Their relationship exploits the natural slope of the site.

HOUSE
Courtyard
Pools
Summerhouse

THE POOLS

The linked pools are the most demanding features in the garden's construction.

THE POOLS AS FEATURES
The pools, with the summerhouse, provide the principal focus of the main garden.

Overflow
Concrete pad
below ground level
Outer skin
Direction of
water flow
Concrete pad
Direction of water flow

HOW THE POOLS WORK
The upper pool feeds the lower pool via an overflow, or waterspill. Water is pumped back to the top pool in a continuous circuit.

Outer skin
also serves as
an informal seat

BUILDING OCTAGONS
The plan of the summerhouse is laid out (above), while the pools are being excavated. The finished pools (below) are set off by the bold outline of a yucca.

THE SUMMERHOUSE

I planned the summerhouse to be the dominant feature of the main garden.

PLANNING THE SUMMERHOUSE
Quaint little garden buildings may be pretty but are impractical – I made sure the summerhouse was large enough to seat several people.

THE SUMMERHOUSE ELEVATION
The roofline of the summerhouse picks up the lines of the building that will be seen beyond it, across the road on the neighbouring site.

GARDEN BUILDINGS

◆ Garden buildings are often too small in plan for their height, making them look ungainly. Disguise this fault by blending buildings into their background through careful planting.

◆ Experiment with wood stains – garden buildings do not have to be standard yellowish-brown.

◆ You may need planning permission for a permanent structure. Check first.

The materials of the summerhouse walls blend with the dry stone walling in the foreground

The octagonal shapes of the pools echo the summerhouse

THE SUMMERHOUSE IN CONTEXT
With the summerhouse and pools built, you can see how the natural slope of the site makes the summerhouse dominant.

THE PLANTING PLAN

BACKING THE DECORATIVE PLANTS are tree and shrub masses that act as the permanent skeleton of the garden, giving it form and structure. They also mould the garden's views by blocking out unwanted features outside it, and they have a third function in sheltering the more tender plants within. I like to think of plants in masses; too many one-offs produce a staccato, restless effect.

VIEWPOINTS
Planting plans should be thought out so that the result looks good from all key viewing points in the garden.

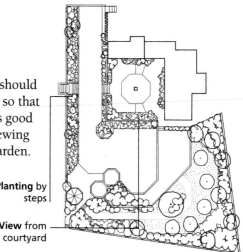

Planting by steps

View from courtyard

THE VIEW FROM THE COURTYARD
Layers of planting, shown below right in the early spring of the garden's second year, step up towards the summerhouse. The lower bed, being a year older than the higher ones, is fuller and more mature. I like to use a generous proportion of evergreen and "evergrey" foliage to give fullness throughout the seasons. Flowers, when they appear, are a bonus.

PLANT DETAILING (BELOW)
At the corner of the steps up to the cherry orchard I set a bold mass of *Euphorbia wulfenii* – an evergreen which is at its best when it shows its spring flowers. The fleshy leaved *Sedum* contrasts with the iris to the left and with the *Stachys* in front. Tall delphiniums, not yet showing, will soften the expanse of new stone walling in the summer.

1 *Cistus corbariensis*
5 *Stachys byzantina*
1 *Taxus baccata*
2 *Libertia grandiflora*
2 *Helleborus foetidus*
2 *Lavandula angustifolia*
3 *Artemisia* 'Powis Castle'
3 *Cistus lusitanicus*

Taxus baccata
Lavandula angustifolia

Iris 'Jane Philips'
Euphorbia wulfenii

5 *Delphinium* mixed (not yet visible)
3 *Euphorbia wulfenii*
1 *Rosa moyesii*
5 *Sedum spectabile*
5 *Iris* 'Jane Philips'
2 *Stachys byzantina*

Mixed planting of perennials and shrubs

Perennials and herbs

Perennials and herbs

Mixed planting of perennials and shrubs

Roses

Decorative shrubs

Perennial infill

Decorative shrubs

Decorative evergreen shrubs

THE MASTER PLAN

The garden includes planting to provide permanent visual structure, act as a screen, and provide shelter. The decorative plants, including shrubs, perennials, roses and herbs (all shown on the tracing paper) overlay the structural planting. The planting of the border by the grass walk is kept quite low to avoid obscuring the view up to the cherry orchard.

Screen hedge

Outbuildings

Grass walk

Sundial

HOUSE

Steps
to cherry
orchard

Mown grass

Small
flowering
trees

Lawn

Rough
grass

Pools

Summerhouse

Evergreen
screening
shrubs

Mown path
through
rough grass

Existing willow

Screening trees
and shrubs

THREE YEARS ON

IT TAKES ABOUT FIVE YEARS for plantings to mature enough to soften the design, producing the right balance between house, garden and setting. These photographs, taken only three years after the planting was complete, nonetheless show my intentions clearly: the garden is approaching early maturity.

THE PLAN
The strength of this plan's design still shows through the overlay of plants.

THE GARDEN FROM THE CHERRY ORCHARD 1
In the foreground you see the steps from the orchard to the long walk. Beyond is the courtyard with its octagonal lawn from which the garden design developed.

THE VIEW FROM THE POOLS 2
From the top pool terrace, the development of the central rose bed and the mixed border on the left is apparent. Planting helps blend in the outbuildings.

THE SUMMERHOUSE 4
From the courtyard (below) or the
long walk, the summerhouse is a
powerful focal point.

THE GARDEN IN ITS SETTING 3
From the orchard there is an
uninterrupted view of the
countryside beyond the planting.

THE COURTYARD PLANTED 5
Planting around the courtyard's
grassed octagon softens and
complements the structural elements.

HARMONY
You can now see how sympathy between new and old materials and building styles integrates the garden with its wider location, and how plants work to soften the composition and meld the garden into a whole.

THE
PLAN
PORTFOLIO

THE PLANS THAT FOLLOW have been chosen to
illustrate many different garden types,
the challenges they pose and the design
solutions available.

KEY TO PLANS

Direction of midday sun   Viewpoint of sketch

1 A SMALL WALLED TOWN GARDEN

A COLLAGE OF RECTANGULAR SHAPES based on the proportions of the conservatory gave rise to a geometrical design with a pool at its centre. The two finial balls set a classical tone, reinforced by the clipped box hedges that impose a strong sense of order on the looser plantings of shrubs behind them.

SITE NOTES

◆ In the lee of a 3m (10ft) wall, this is a sheltered, warm site.

◆ There are only two access points – a gate on the left, and the conservatory.

◆ The design brief calls for a water feature and a bench, to be given a classical-style interpretation.

◆ With so much going on in quite a small space – approximately 9 x 7m (30 x 23ft) – there is a risk of untidiness so grid selection will be crucial.

Gateway

Shrub planting
to soften wall

Finial ball
set on column

Paths
in consolidated
gravel

3m (10ft)
wall

Pool
with stone
stepping pad

Informal planting
in gravel areas

Clipped box tree
for formal, classical
effect

Clipped box
hedging

Brick edging
to gravel path

Old stone
edging
to pool

Position for
bench

Clipped box hedging

Finial ball
set on
column

Shrub planting
to soften walls

Side wall

Stone paving

Conservatory
shape (quartered)
forms the basic
module for the grid

Conservatory

HOUSE

THE GRID SQUARE was
taken off the corner of
the conservatory.

0   3   6   ft
| | |

0   1   2   m

2 AN ENCLOSED SIDE GARDEN

THE SCALE OF THIS GARDEN derives from the large piece of statuary which is its focus and which is carefully related in scale to the high wall behind it. The garden is softened by a selection of shade-loving plants in the shadow of the back wall and brightened by colourful exotics in the sunny areas.

VIEW DOWN THE GARDEN, showing how the urn works as a focal point against the high boundary wall.

SITE NOTES

◆ The site is squeezed between the house and the garage and measures approximately 16 x 13m (52 x 43ft).

◆ Given its aspect and the 3m (10ft) high wall that forms its far boundary, this is a warm enclosure, though the foot of the wall is permanently shaded.

◆ Access from the gateways to the garden – one the entrance from the road, the other on the path leading to the garage – will need to be accommodated.

Compost area
screened by shrubs

Shrub planting
to soften high wall

Shade-loving shrubs
in lee of wall

3m (10ft) wall

Garage wall

New tree
to break line of back wall

Shade-loving shrubs
soften garage wall

Feature urn
(see sketch
above)

Lawn

Shrub planting

Existing tree

Stone path

Planting beds
in gravelled area (full sun)

Gateway
from garage

Brick edging
to gravelled area

Stone terrace
sitting/eating area

HOUSE

Brick step
up to terrace

Hedge

Existing tree
establishes corner
boundary

Greenhouse

Kitchen

Stone path

Gateway
from road

```
0   3   6   9      ft
|___|___|___|___|

0   1   2   3      m
|___|___|___|___|
```

3 A RECTANGULAR SUBURBAN SITE

THIS TYPICAL RECTANGULAR PLOT is at the rear of a suburban house. Evolving the design at 45° to the house adds an illusion of width, which is reinforced by breaking the site into a sequence of individual "rooms" defined by plant masses, brick edging and contrasting surfaces. Though the design actually consists of formal square areas, a meandering effect is created.

Existing tree

Consolidated gravel contrasts with adjacent brick

Storage shed hidden by planting

Brick seating terrace to catch afternoon sun

Existing hedge retained

Planting of shrubs for autumn/winter colour

Step made of bricks laid on edge

Existing hedge

Brick edge/step

Paving slabs

Fountain

Cobbled area

Paving to side access

Lawn

Lawn

Herb garden convenient for kitchen

Kitchen

Step made of bricks laid on edge

Mixed planting

Brick-laid terrace for morning sun

Fence

Door

Door

HOUSE

BLOCK PLAN showing the interlocking shapes from which the garden is designed.

0 3 6 9 ft
0 1 2 3 m

4 A GARDEN IN A HOLLOW

BUILDING A RETAINING WALL toward the perimeter allows the part of the garden closest to the house to be levelled. The wall is made thicker to provide seating near the summerhouse, whose shape is echoed in the central bed and picked up in the lines of the terrace and both lawns. Defined geometrical shapes such as this tend to work well in small gardens, where loose curves often look weak.

SITE NOTES

◆ The garden rises by more than a metre (3ft) to the back wall and side wall to the left of the house.

◆ The octagonal summerhouse is the dominant feature of both the side and rear gardens. It is an obvious shape to develop into the design.

◆ The brief includes a requirement to maximize the lawn and terrace areas.

LOOKING TOWARD the boundary pier and brick wall, showing the brick seat and summerhouse.

5 A SCREENED GARDEN

SCREENING OUT THE NEIGHBOURS is more easily said than done – an obvious screen makes one wonder what is behind it. The solution here is to draw the eye into the site with the heavy patterning of flower beds set into the run of brick paving; shrubs and perennials will be able to flop over the terracing without impeding the lawnmower. The ornamental tree by the entrance to the parking area acts as a secondary focus.

SITE NOTES

◆ The neighbouring properties on two sides are very close to the boundaries of this site and will need further screening with trees and shrubs. Additionally, the design must create features that will draw the eye and hold it within the site.

◆ The owners want the centre of the garden to remain as lawn: the eye-holding features will therefore have to be set off to the sides.

Existing trees provide some screening of neighbouring buildings

Shrubs to screen garden wall

Fruit trees

Hedge behind shrubs

Deciduous trees

Shrub planting to screen wall and house beyond

Ornamental tree marks entrance

Brick path to main terrace

Compost area

Garden shed

Flowers planted in gravelled area act as focal point

Mixed borders

Brick terracing unifies design

Lawn

PARKING AREA

Existing trees

```
0   6   12  18  24  30  ft
|   |   |   |   |   |
|   |   |   |   |   |
0   2   4   6   8   10  m
```

Existing tree

HOUSE

Planted tubs

Doors to terrace

Stone terrace

Sculpture feature set in small lawn

THE HONEYCOMB of flower beds on the left focuses the garden pattern.

6 AN URBAN CORNER SITE

THE HOUSE HAS A FORMAL FACADE, but the garden's shape is irregular and anything but formal. Squaring up the lawn and terrace goes some way to reconcile the two, with a new tree to create a line of vision from the house. From the new seating area the focus is the large tree, with the pool as a counterpoint.

SITE NOTES

◆ The plot is dominated by a large deciduous tree on the right flank.

◆ The owners require a lawn and a paddling pool for their children. They also wish to have a new seating area on the left side of the garden where they can enjoy the sun.

◆ A line of vision needs to be created from the house and another from the new seating area: the large tree is an obvious focal point for the latter.

THE LARGE TREE is balanced by areas of interest created at lower levels in the garden.

0 3 6 9 ft

0 1 2 3 m

Existing trees

New tree to culminate view from house

Trellis screen

Sculpture

Brick seating wall

Paddling pool

Water planting

Shrub planting to soften wall

Dominant existing tree

Brick seating wall

Shrubs to screen fence

Slab paving seating area

New seating area (brick-paved)

New trees

Lawn

Planted tubs

Doors to terrace

HOUSE

Brick-paved shaded seating area

55

7 A GARDEN WITH AN OPEN VIEW

THE LINE OF THE STEPS down from the terrace to the lawn radiates from the raised pool, which is the centre of the pattern, and directs the eye toward the break in the hedge that reveals the paddock and horses. The planting on the two right-hand boundaries provides valuable wind shelter.

SITE NOTES

◆ The house and garden are in a fairly exposed position quite near the sea and are regularly blasted by strong sea winds. Sheltering screens of shrubs and/or hedges are desirable.

◆ To the left of the garden is a paddock, and the owners wish to incorporate a view of it into the garden. A low, slatted fence will be included to accommodate this.

◆ An extensive paved terrace is needed for outdoor entertaining.

THE PATTERN underlying this garden's design is strongly based on radiating curves.

PADDOCK

Raised pool is the centre of the pattern

Ground cover planting

Low, slatted fence to permit view through to paddock

Hedge

Shrub planting against fence

Perennials in front of shrubs

Rough grass planted with bulbs

Existing trees

Hedge

Rough grass

Path to stable

Perennials

Radiating steps with planting spaces

Hedge to break prevailing sea winds

Shrubbery with screening hedge behind

Way through to tennis court

Mown lawn

HOUSE

```
0   6   12  18  24  30  ft
|   |   |   |   |   |
0   2   4   6   8   10 m
```

Brick terrace for outdoor entertaining

Hedge

THE PLAN PORTFOLIO

8 A COUNTRY COURTYARD

THREE CHANGES OF LEVEL are incorporated in this squared layout and the collage of patterns is made up of old stone, granite setts (paving blocks) and planting of mainly culinary herbs. The areas of paving are punctuated with wooden tubs planted with bright annuals for summer colour.

SITE NOTES

◆ Old farm buildings on either side of the courtyard are to be retained.

◆ Though it has an unfavourable aspect, the site is enclosed by buildings and walls and is therefore very well sheltered.

◆ The garden slopes up from the house to the gate – steps will resolve this.

Existing tree

Shrub planting to soften wall

Sculpture to focus view from the house

Perimeter wall

Granite setts

Stone slabs

Gate to parking area

Step up

Shrubs

Step up

Granite setts

Herbs and roses

Wall of old farm building

HOUSE

Shrub planting

Wall of old farm building

Herbs and roses

Stone terrace

Tubs planted with annuals for summer colour

Kitchen door

```
0   3   6   9   12  ft
0   1   2   3   4   m
```

THE GRID underlying this layout was based on the proportions of the house, then subdivided into smaller areas.

9 A SQUARE SUBURBAN PLOT

THE BULL'S-EYE PATTERN makes the central pool a powerful feature to hold the eye within the site (there is a very limited view). Such a strong geometric design needs a fairly wide site and works only if heavily over-planted. Surplus soil from the excavation of the pool is used to build up the border at the end of the garden. When planted with trees and evergreens, this will help block out traffic noise as well.

SITE NOTES

◆ The location is very enclosed, with only a limited outlook. The eye must therefore be held within the site by a strong design feature.

◆ The available view should be optimized by the design.

◆ Traffic noise can be a nuisance in this garden: the design must help reduce it.

THIS PATTERN contrasts modernity in layout with very soft planting designed to encourage birds.

```
0   3   6   9   12    ft
|   |   |   |   |
0   1   2   3   4     m
```

Contoured mound helps reduce traffic noise

Decorative trees act as ornamental screen

Pool is central feature

Lawn at same level as terrace

Low fence to reveal view

Shrubs

Trees

Gravel area slopes down to pool edge

Terrace retaining wall

Terrace slab paving

Side gate

Contoured mound with tree

Shrubs to soften corner

Shrub planting

Informal planting in gravel

Wall to retain terrace level and contain water planting

Bog planting

Decorative trees mirroring those in the opposite corner

Brick seat with wooden top

HOUSE

10 A SPLIT-LEVEL GARDEN

MANY OLDER TERRACED HOUSES have rear gardens that are approached from a basement area subsequently opened out to increase light to a remodelled kitchen. The first task here is to improve the basement seating area. The second is to angle the lawn-level pattern so that the terrace faces the sun. The third is to fix the eye with a levelled area as a feature in the bank created by surplus soil at the end.

THE VIEW down into the garden from a tall town house can vary greatly according to which floor you look from: the design should take this into account.

Existing tree

Shrubs
to disguise
end fence

Sculpture feature
to draw the eye

Bank of soil

Raised gravelled area
with informal planting

Large pots
attract the eye

Brick seating area
facing afternoon sun

Shrubs

Lawn

Fence
masked by shrubs

Brick edging
to lawn

Climbers

Flight of steps
from lower
terrace to upper
garden

HOUSE

Kitchen door

Retaining wall

Barbecue area

Brick lower terrace
with stone slabs
interspersed

0   3   6   ft
0   1   2   m

SITE NOTES

◆ Surplus soil dug out when the basement area was extended was dumped at the end of the garden. This needs to be tidied into a secondary level of the main garden with a feature to draw the eye.

◆ A seating area will have to be constructed to face the direction of the sun.

◆ Access is from the basement only – there are no steps down from the raised ground floor of the house.

11 A RIVERSIDE TERRACE

THIS TERRACE WITH A RIVER VIEW is severely overlooked by a neighbouring building. Strong ground detailing with a small water feature and a pergola all deflect the eye from the neighbouring property. For maximum impact the pergola is sited where the vertical and horizontal axes meet and its octagonal design reflects the pattern of the bay windows looking on to the garden. Planting tall shrubs behind the pergola strengthens the concept.

SITE NOTES

◆ The terrace has an excellent river view, but its enjoyment is spoiled by a tall neighbouring building, which overlooks the terrace to the point of domination.

◆ An unplanted gravel area at the foot of the garden is needed to provide an unrestricted view across the river.

RIVER

Gravelled viewing area (part of an octagon)

Octagonal brick terrace

Conifer hedge

Steps up

Gravel with informal planting

Brick paving

Pergola (see sketch above)

Fountain

Shrubs low-growing, so as not to obscure the river view

Steps up (part of an octagon)

Brick edging to rough grass bank

Lawn shaped to form part of an octagon

Shrub planting

Stone steps

Rough grass bank sloping down to lawn

Gravelled area

Brick terrace

OVERLOOKING BUILDINGS

HOUSE

Bay windows give rise to octagonal patterns used in the garden design

A VIEW along the new brick-paved terrace toward the pergola and water feature.

```
0    6    12   18   ft
|    |    |    |
0    2    4    6    m
```

12 A SEASIDE FRONT GARDEN

A WINDBREAK does not make a successful feature, however well it serves its purpose, in a garden of ordinary size. The visual impact of this plan for a windy coastal garden comes from a strong ground pattern, expressed in brick, grass and gravel, stepping up three times to the front door. Planted pots on a brick pad in the gravel provide a focus from the street entry as well as from the house.

Mixed planting

Shrub planting
to soften wall

Hedge
(windbreak)

Wall
(windbreak)

Shrubs
to soften wall

Lawn

Planted pots
on brick pad

Gravelled area
with loose planting

Granite sett edging

Tiled threshold

Perennials

Brick paving
level 3

Brick paving
level 2

Entrance

Garden entrance
from driveway

Brick paving
level 1

HOUSE

Shrub planting

A STRONG GROUND PATTERN works with the house's proportions to create interest. The layout allows a wide approach to the front door.

SITE NOTES

◆ The aspect is very windy, so a windbreak of a wall backed by a hedge or shrubs is essential. The windbreak must not become oppressive however – even in this modest space it will be necessary to create interest within the plot.

◆ The bold windows that dominate the house are the basis for the grid.

13 AN ANGULAR GARDEN

USING A SIMPLE GEOMETRY deriving from the plan of the house, the rear garden resolves itself into a paved forecourt, brick terrace and lawn, bounded by low shrubs that will not obscure the attractive view beyond. Side areas are maximized by levelling near the house and pushing the rising ground back behind retaining walls, and a path is created to zigzag through the stepped-up border.

SITE NOTES

◆ The rear of the house looks out to a fine view, which should be emphasized.

◆ Both the front garden and the areas to the sides of the house rise towards the boundaries of the site. These will need retaining to create some level space.

0 6 12 18 ft
0 2 4 6 m

Boundary fence

Existing trees

Hedge

Site for bench

Slab path zigzags through loosely planted gravel

Pergola beams

Retaining wall

Low retaining wall

Perennial borders with slab path between

Gravelled area

Perimeter wall

THE REAR GARDEN is simplified so as not to distract the eye from the view beyond.

Rear garden

Low shrubs do not obscure the view

Rear garden

Terrace brick pattern contrasts with forecourt

Screen wall

Gateway

Brick steps

Climbers covering wall

Covered porch

Entrance forecourt (brick-paved)

Slab path

Entrance to forecourt

Retaining wall

Shrub planting

Lawn

HOUSE

14 A BANKED GARDEN

THE FIRST TASK is to extend the lower terrace by pushing the bank back behind a retaining brick wall. This allows for improved access by new steps to the upper level, where a new second terrace takes advantage of the view down over the cottage.

THE SHELTERED paved terrace at the lower level of the garden.

SITE NOTES

◆ The cottage nestles into the grass banks that surround it. The garden proper is on a level with the rooms on the first floor of the cottage.

◆ The lower terrace, protected by the bank on two sides, and by the cottage on the remaining sides, is remarkably sheltered and sunny.

◆ Lawnmower access needs to be provided from the rear garden past the side of the cottage to the front lawn (not shown).

Rear boundary hedge

Building screened by hedge

Hedge

Planting beds in gravel surrounds

Feature

Grass bank

Mixed planting

0 3 6 9 12 15 18 ft
0 1 2 3 4 5 6 m

Steps up to higher level

Upper terrace in stone, with view down over cottage

Shrubs

Stone path

Lawn

Lawn

Shrub planting on bank

Retaining wall formed by extending step risers

Bank

Steps linking lower terrace with upper garden

Secondary steps to upper garden

Grass bank

Grassed access to front garden for lawnmower

Extended lower terrace paved with stone

Steps up

COTTAGE

15 A ROAD-SIDE GARDEN SCREENED

WHEN IT WAS FIRST LAID OUT in the early 1900s, this garden was set out to lead from the house to the top right-hand boundary. Now, to avoid noise from the road beyond the left-hand boundary, it makes sense to create a new principal terrace right of the house's projecting wing in full afternoon sun, looking on to the formal flower garden and across to the existing trees.

SITE NOTES

◆ The road beyond the left-hand boundary has become noisy. An alternative seating area is required where the noise will be less intrusive.

◆ A shrub screen on the boundary with the road will reduce noise and shelter the garden from wind.

◆ A substantial asset of the existing garden is the fine group of large trees.

THE VIEW from the extended terrace by the house across the formal flower garden to the summerhouse.

Shrub screen against road noise and prevailing winds

Existing large trees

Steps down to flower garden and lawns

Summerhouse

Orchard planting

New formal beds in gravel surround

Rough grass under trees planted with bulbs

Lawn

Mixed small trees and shrubs

Existing tree

Steps up to terrace

Lawn

Original brick-paved terrace

Boundary hedge

New extension to terrace shielded from road noise by projecting wing of the house

HOUSE

ROAD

Entrance to house

0   9   18   27   36   ft

0   3   6   9   12   m

16 A GARDEN FOR A FORMER STABLE

TO HOLD THE EYE WITHIN THE SITE a simple round lily pool is made the focal point of sweeping circular patterns, defined by yew and shrub hedging that helps to obscure the garden buildings in the top right-hand corner and conceal the driveway. The sun terrace, positioned to give a view back to the cottage, a converted former stable, functions as part of this pattern.

SITE NOTES

◆ The former stable – now a cottage – is a pretty building with a graceful church spire behind it. A terrace should be created to take advantage of this view.

◆ Other aspects from the garden are not especially attractive, so the eye needs to be retained within the site.

THE PATTERN of strong curves gives a sense of enclosure and focuses the eye on the central pool.

Gravel driveway

Existing tree

Screen of shrubs and small trees

Garden shed

Garage

Mixed borders

Sun terrace

Yew hedging

Greenhouse

Screening hedge

Lawn

Water irises

Lily pond

Yew hedging

Gravel path continues driveway

Row of pleached trees

Screening trees

Gravel path

Brick-paved terrace

COTTAGE

Boundary hedge

0 9 18 27 36 ft

0 3 6 9 12 m

17 A SMALL COURTYARD DESIGN

AN UPPER POOL TRICKLING INTO A LOWER ONE makes the feature, emphasized by a piece of sculpture, that holds the eye in the courtyard rather than allowing it to follow the lines of the existing large deciduous tree upwards. Low brick walls retain most of the plantings at the edges of the site and provide casual seating. The brick paving matches the retaining walls, but the scheme is made less formal by introducing stone slabs.

SITE NOTES

◆ The large deciduous tree dominates the space and draws the eye upward. A strong feature is necessary to hold the eye down.

◆ The natural site for a feature is by the base of the tree, where it will be seen from the house, studio and gate.

◆ Paved space is required for eating outdoors in summer.

0 1 2 3 4 5 ft
0 0.5 1 1.5 m

Mixed planting
in raised bed

Feature tree

Seating area
is brick-paved, with
occasional stone slabs to
relieve the formality

Brick retaining wall
serves also for
seating

STUDIO

Informal planting
in brick cut-out

Low retaining wall

Door
from studio to
courtyard

Gate
to courtyard

Existing
large deciduous
tree

Shrubs

Raised bed
planted with
shrubs

Stone slabs
stepped down

Upper
pool

Plinth
for intended
sculpture

Door
from house
to courtyard

Lower pool

HOUSE

Raised brick
surround

Mixed shrub planting
in ground-level bed

Stone slab
acts as water course,
joining the pools

THE VERTICALS of the tree contrast with the horizontal planes of the water feature.

18 A PRIVATE TOWN GARDEN

CREATING PRIVACY IN A SMALL TOWN GARDEN is a classic garden design challenge. A light, skeletal metal arbour beneath an existing tree provides some screening from tall neighbouring houses. The eye is drawn to this structure across a foreground pattern of paving and gravel planted with herbs and roses, and evergreens for winter interest in the shade.

THE NEW STRUCTURE as it appears from the ground floor rear rooms of the house.

Large tree grows through open roof of new structure and shelters eating area

New structure

Upper pool

Step up to eating area

Waterspill to lower level

Lower pool

Planted pots with annual colour

Stone paving

Mixed planting with roses prominent

Gravel area with sun-loving plants

Alternative eating and seating area

Eating area surfaced with gravel

Statue acts as alternative focus to metal structure beyond

Step

Stone-paved area

Site for bench

Evergreens for winter interest

Retaining wall

French windows opening from kitchen

HOUSE

Planted pots with annual colour

Steps from basement area to ground floor level

Garden door from ground floor

0 3 6 9 12 15 ft
0 1 2 3 4 5 m

SITE NOTES

◆ The owners' requirement was for space to entertain on summer evenings, but the evening sun falls only at the end of the plot, which is in full view of the neighbours. The solution is to provide an arbour-like structure.

◆ Access needs to be provided to the garden from the basement kitchen, below garden level, and from the raised ground floor.

19 A COUNTRY HOUSE WITH A VIEW

THE HOUSE IS STONE-BUILT, so the terraces to the front and rear are specified to match. Similarly, the gravel used on the forecourt is of the same material as the house. So that the view into parkland is unobscured, a ha-ha (concealed ditch) is used to mark that boundary. The rear is made into a lawn with shrub screens at the sides only.

SITE NOTES

◆ This house has fine views over an 18th-century park to the rear. A ha-ha (concealed ditch) would make a suitable boundary.

◆ As it is a retirement home, a low-maintenance scheme is most appropriate – lawns and gravel.

◆ Screen planting will be required to give wind shelter as well as privacy on the left-hand side of the garden.

◆ Existing trees on the entrance side of the house work well with its elevations and aspect.

THE VIEW is left completely open into the parkland beyond the garden.

ADJACENT PARKLAND

Ha-ha (concealed ditch)

Stone seat (see sketch) in sunny corner with view over park

Shrub screening to act as windbreak

Lawn

Brick edging

Sculpture

Tubs planted for summer colour

Stone terrace

0 6 12 18 24 30 ft
0 2 4 6 8 m

HOUSE

Gravel path

Entrance to stone terrace

Existing tree

Shrub planting to act as windbreak

Stone step

Compost area with shrub screen

Garden shed

Garage

Existing tree

Lawn with fruit trees

Low stone walls

Entrance from road

Gravel forecourt

Brick edging

Existing tree

20 AN EASY-CARE TOWN GARDEN

TO MAKE A LARGER AREA of terracing, set the lawn at an angle; this gives the additional benefit of a hard surface leading from the house to the rear gate without the need to devise a separate path. The pergola helps to create a feeling of being *in* the site rather than on it – it will take three or four years to get sufficient greenery to couch the garden. A bed of annuals would be an alternative to the pool, making a very strong central statement and holding the eye firmly in the site.

SITE NOTES

◆ This is the owners' first home. It is newly built and the site is barren.

◆ The requirement is for a garden with plenty of space to sunbathe (the garden is sunny) and eat out, with a minimum of maintenance – the owners are first-time gardeners. Therefore generous terracing and a small lawn seem appropriate.

Rear gate
access to garage

Feature tree

Garage wall

Gravelled area
with brick edging

| 0 | 2 | 4 | 6 | 8 | ft |
| 0 | 0.5 1 | 1.5 | 2 | 2.5 | m |

Mixed shrub and
tree planting

Lawn

Boundary fence

Mixed planting
of shrubs and perennials

Brick edging

Pool set
in lawn

Fountain

Slab-paved terrace

Informal
planting
of sun-loving
plants

Side access

Pergola
helps keep the
eye down,
within the site

Informal planting
against house

HOUSE

Side access

A SQUARE within a
square provides a
simple block plan.

69

21 A COUNTRY HOUSE IN WOODLAND

WITH A GLORIOUS LANDSCAPE as its surround, a garden need do no more than set the house in its environs. On the upper side therefore, decking and terracing lead down to lawns that swoop away to the tops of trees on the banks below. Wild flowers are planted in shaped areas of rough grass to the sides of the garden. The patterns of the layout are geometrical, like those of the house, but abstracted and extended to blend into the countryside.

SITE NOTES

◆ The house is positioned on a hillside and enjoys views over magnificent rolling, wooded country. The trees and contours of the natural landscape must condition the design.

◆ Planting should be kept modest in scale and used to link the house into the landscape. The most important plants already on the site are the trees, some of which are very large.

Gravelled area

Deck

Sculpture

Huge trees dominate the site

Paved area

Tops of smaller trees are at lawn level

Larger trees partially obscure view, adding perspective

Ground falls away sharply beyond lawn

Vegetable garden

Lawn

HOUSE

Lawn

Driveway

Entrance to house

Brick path

Paved area

Dog pen

Orchard

Garage

Screen planting of shrubs

Rough grass under trees

Herb garden

Barn

| 0 | 9 | 18 | 27 | 36 | ft |
| 0 | 3 | 6 | 9 | 12 | m |

SITE DETAIL

THE TERRACES are designed to work with the rooms they adjoin. The deck, for example, to be used for outdoor entertaining, is outside the reception room; similarly, the breakfast terrace and herb garden are close to the kitchen. The shapes of the terraces were determined partly by practicality (the deck should have both sun and shade), but also by the need to harmonize with the contours of the garden.

A PROJECTION demonstrates more clearly than a plan could the different levels in a complex design such as this.

Gravelled area leading to lawn

Reception room

Deck

Shrubs

Paved area

Kitchen

Shrubs

Sculpture

Table and seats built round base of tree

Vegetable garden

HOUSE

Gravel forecourt

Entrance to house

Breakfast terrace paved in brick

Herb garden

0	3	6	9	ft
0	1	2	3	m

INDEX

ACKNOWLEDGMENTS

John Brookes:
I would like to credit everyone who helped me in this production – though small, it was complicated.

My long-suffering editor and art editor at Dorling Kindersley, Rosie and Carole. Michael Zinn, my assistant, who acted both as a competent draughtsperson and liaison between all parties, and lastly, my secretary, Jill Robertson-Macdonald, who from time to time mops my brow and types my texts. I thank them all.

Dorling Kindersley:
Carole Ash, Managing Art Editor; Rosie Pearson, Managing Editor; Karen Ward, Art Editor; Susannah Marriott, Senior Editor; Lorna Damms, Editor; Maryann Rogers, Production Manager; Karen Ruane, DTP Designer; Pippa Ward, Secretarial Assistant

Photography:
Studio photography pages 18-29 Ray Gaffney
Location photography pages 30-48 John Brookes
Additional photography Steve Gorton page 39cl, Tim Ridley page 1, Dave King page 5cl
Photographs page 5c, cb, cr, rb Carole Ash
Hand model Kate Scott

Page 7cl Bauhaus-Archiv, Berlin
Page 7tr Pier Gallery, Stromness, Orkney

Illustration:
Plans pages 50-71 Joe Robinson
Working plans and sketches John Brookes and Michael Zinn
Symbols for information boxes Sarah Ponder

Index: Leigh Priest